PETERSBURG
National Military Park, Virginia

by Richard Wayne Lykes

NATIONAL PARK SERVICE HISTORICAL HANDBOOK SERIES NO. 13

Washington, D. C., 1951

(Reprint 1961)

The National Park System, of which this area is a unit, is dedicated to conserving the scenic, scientific, and historic heritage of the United States for the benefit and inspiration of its people.

PETERSBURG

National Military Park - Virginia

By Richard Wayne Lykes

All rights reserved, which include the right to reproduce this book or portions thereof in any form except provided by U.S. Copyright Laws.

Digital Scanning and Publishing is a leader in the electronic republication of historical books and documents. We publish many of our titles as eBooks, paperback and hardcover editions. DSI is committed to bringing many traditional and well-known books back to life, retaining the look and feel of the original work.

Trade Paperback ISBN: 1-58218-783-5

©2010 DSI Digital Reproduction
First DSI Printing: May 2010

Published by Digital Scanning Inc. Scituate, MA 02066 781-545-2100 http://www.Digitalscanning.com and http://www.PDFLibrary.com

Contents

	Page
THE UNION STRATEGY OF 1864	2
THE STRATEGIC IMPORTANCE OF PETERSBURG	4
THE BATTLE OF PETERSBURG, JUNE 15–18, 1864	8
FIRST UNION ATTEMPT ON THE WELDON RAILROAD	11
THE BATTLE OF THE CRATER, JULY 30, 1864	12
THE FIGHT FOR THE WELDON RAILROAD	22
UNION ENCIRCLEMENT CONTINUES	25
THE SOUTH STRIKES BACK—THE BATTLE OF FORT STEDMAN	34
UNION ENCIRCLEMENT BECOMES A REALITY	39
THE FALL OF THE CITY	43
GUIDE TO THE AREA	46
HOW TO REACH THE PARK	55
ADMINISTRATION	56
RELATED AREAS	56
VISITOR FACILITIES	56

TABLE OF EVENTS

I. EVENTS IN 1864 PRECEDING THE CAMPAIGN

Mar. 9. U. S. Grant made commander in chief of the Union armies.
May 4. Butler and the Army of the James capture City Point, Virginia.
May 5–7. Battle of the Wilderness.
May 8–19. Battle of Spotsylvania Court House.
May 23. Battle of North Anna River.
May 29. Battle of Totopotomoy Creek.
June 3. Battle of Cold Harbor.
June 9. Raid by Union cavalry on Petersburg lines.

II. EVENTS IN 1864 DURING THE CAMPAIGN

June 15–18. Opening Battle of Petersburg.
June 22–23. Union attack on Weldon Railroad repulsed.
July 30. Battle of the Crater.
Aug. 18–21. Union forces capture the Weldon Railroad.
Aug. 25. Battle of Reams Station.
Sept. 14–17. Hampton's cavalry raid on Union beef supply.
Sept. 29–Oct. 1. Battle of Peebles' Farm and Capture of Fort Harrison.
Oct. 19. Battle of Cedar Creek.
Oct. 27. Battle of Burgess' Mill.

III. EVENTS IN 1865 DURING THE CAMPAIGN

Feb. 5–7. Battle of the Boydton Plank Road.
Mar. 25. Battle of Fort Stedman.
Apr. 1. Battle of Five Forks.
Apr. 2. General Union attacks on Confederate lines outside Petersburg.
Apr. 3. Union troops enter Richmond and Petersburg.
Apr. 9. Lee and the Army of Northern Virginia surrender at Appomattox Court House.

In the final year of the Civil War in the East, the fighting centered upon Petersburg, an important supply depot for the Richmond area. After 10 months of combat, both from behind prepared positions and along the main routes of supply, the Confederates were forced to give up Petersburg and Richmond on April 2, 1865. One week later Lee surrendered the Army of Northern Virginia at Appomattox Court House.

By June of 1864, the Civil War lay heavily on both the North and the South. For more than 3 years the two antagonists—the Blue and the Gray—had struggled to determine the fate of the Union.

The capitals of the embattled forces stood only 110 miles apart. But these miles of rolling Virginia countryside which separated Richmond from Washington had proven exceedingly difficult for the Union forces to cross. Various Northern generals had been placed in command of the Army of the Potomac and had faced Lee's Army of Northern Virginia. So far not one had been successful in destroying Lee's army or in capturing Richmond.

Perhaps Gen. George B. McClellan had come the closest to success when in the late spring and early summer of 1862 the Northern troops had threatened the Confederate capital, only to be repulsed on the outskirts. The other Northern commanders who followed McClellan, such as Pope, Burnside, and Hooker, were less successful. Their drives had been met and turned aside by Lee, the able Southern guardian of Richmond.

After 36 months of bitter conflict the war in the East seemed, to many observers, to be far from a final settlement. The failure of Union forces to deliver a decisive blow against the Army of Northern Virginia was a source of growing concern in Washington. The Confederacy, for its part, was no more successful in settling the issue. Attempted invasions of the Northern States by Lee were turned back at Antietam in September 1862 and at Gettysburg in July 1863.

FRONTISPIECE: *View of Petersburg in 1865 looking south across the Appomattox River.* Courtesy, National Archives.

Lt. Gen. Ulysses S. Grant, Union commander at Petersburg. Courtesy, National Archives.

Gen. Robert E. Lee, Confederate commander at Petersburg. Courtesy, National Archives.

Farther west the picture was brighter for Northern hopes. In the same month as the Battle of Gettysburg, the town of Vicksburg, Miss., fell into Union hands. A few days later, July 9, 1863, Port Hudson, the last remaining stronghold of the Confederacy on the banks of the Mississippi River, surrendered. Later in 1863, the Union capture of Chattanooga, Tenn., threw open the gateway to Georgia and South Carolina.

Strategically, despite the stalemate in Virginia, the beginning of 1864 found the Northern armies in a stronger position than the Confederate military forces. Not only was there a distinct possibility that the South could be split into two parts, but the greater resources at the command of the Lincoln administration were beginning to count more heavily with each passing day. All that seemed to be needed to end the war was an able Union commander who could marshal the mighty resources of his country for a last tremendous blow at the South. Such a man was found in Gen. Ulysses S. Grant, the victor at Vicksburg and Chattanooga, who was made commander in chief of all the Union armies on March 9, 1864.

The Union Strategy of 1864

To accomplish the conquest of the Confederacy the Northern plan called for a huge two-pronged attack. Gen. William T. Sherman was in command of the southern prong which was assigned the task of capturing Atlanta, marching to the sea, and then turning north to effect a junction with Grant. Opposed to Sherman was the Army of Tennessee led by Gen. Joseph E. Johnston.

It was the upper arm of the movement which was directly concerned with Richmond and Petersburg. This was composed of two armies: the Army of the Potomac and the Army of the James. It was the task of these armies to capture Richmond, crush the Army of Northern Virginia, and march south toward Sherman.

The story of the Army of the James in the early phase of the offensive may be briefly told. Gen. Benjamin F. Butler was ordered to advance upon Richmond from the south and threaten communications between the Confederate capital and the Southern States. With some 40,000 Union troops the advance was begun. City Point, located at the junction of the James and Appomattox Rivers and soon to be the supply center for the attack on Petersburg, was captured on May 4, 1864. Within 2 weeks, however, a numerically inferior Confederate force shut up the Army of the James, "as if it had been in a bottle strongly corked," in Bermuda Hundred, a loop formed by the winding James and Appomattox Rivers. Here Butler waited, while north of him the Army of the Potomac and the Army of Northern Virginia engaged in a series of bloody battles.

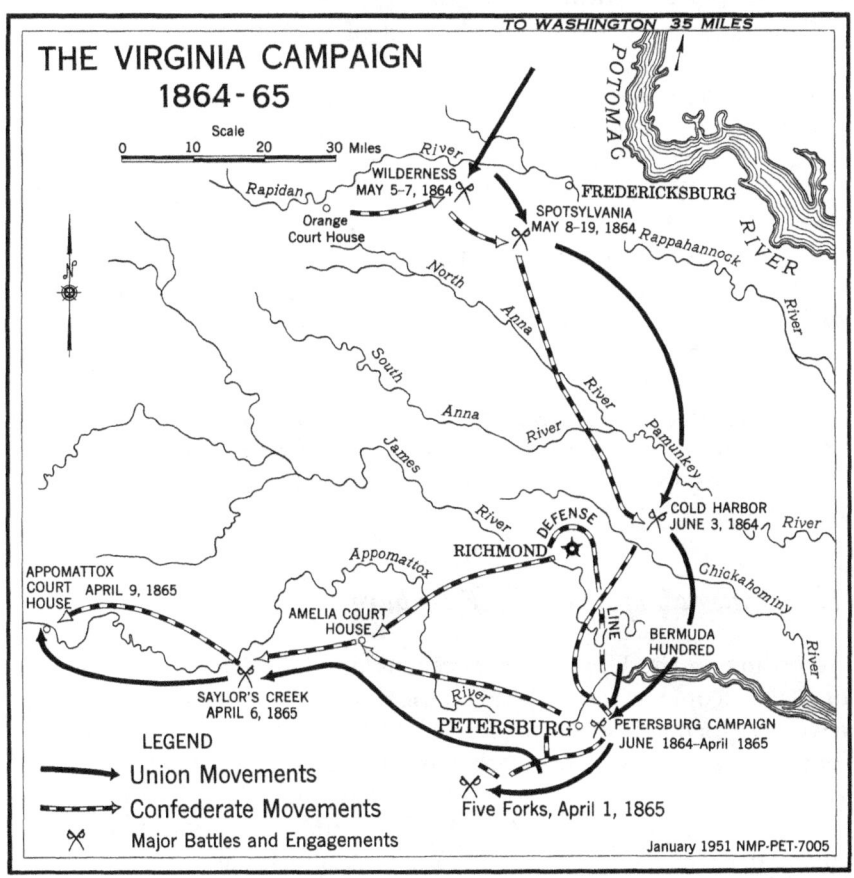

The Battle of the Wilderness, May 5–7, 1864, began what proved to be the start of the final campaign against the Army of Northern Virginia. Here the Army of the Potomac, commanded by Gen. George G. Meade and numbering approximately 118,000 troops, fought the Confederate defenders of Richmond. Lee had about 62,000 men with him, while an additional 30,000 under Gen. P. G. T. Beauregard held the Richmond-Petersburg area. The battle resulted in a fearful loss of men on both sides, although the armies remained intact. This was followed by an equally heavy series of engagements around Spotsylvania Court House from May 8 to 19.

Failing to destroy the Army of Northern Virginia in these battles, Grant moved the Army of the Potomac to the east of Richmond. It was his hope that he would outflank the Confederate defenders by persistent night marches. Lee was not to be so easily outguessed, however, and after minor battles at the North Anna River (May 23) and Totopotomoy Creek (May 29), Grant arrived at Cold Harbor, about 8 miles east of Richmond. Between him and that city stood Lee's army. On June 3, 2 days after he arrived at Cold Harbor, Grant ordered a direct frontal assault. He was repulsed with heavy losses.

This was the situation at the end of the first month of Grant's campaign:

1. Both sides had suffered heavy casualties. The approximate percentage of casualties to total strength, including reinforcements, was 31 percent for the North and 32 percent for the South.

2. The ability of the Union to refill the depleted ranks was greater than that of the Confederacy.

3. The offensive strength of Lee had been sapped. From the time of the Battle of Spotsylvania Court House until the end of the war, except for local, small-scale actions, the Army of Northern Virginia was a defensive weapon only. This Army, although hurt, had not been crushed, and the Confederate flag still waved over Richmond.

In June, after Cold Harbor, Grant decided to turn quickly to the south of Richmond and isolate the city and the defending troops by cutting the railroads which supplied it. To do this he would need to attack Petersburg.

The Strategic Importance of Petersburg

According to the United States census of 1860, Petersburg was a city of 18,266 people. It was situated on the southern bank of the Appomattox River less than 8 miles from City Point, the place where the Appomattox joins the James; 23 miles north was Richmond. As the war progressed and the territory to the north and east was shut off, Richmond became increasingly dependent on Petersburg for supplies. Through it passed a constant stream of war materials and necessities of life from the South

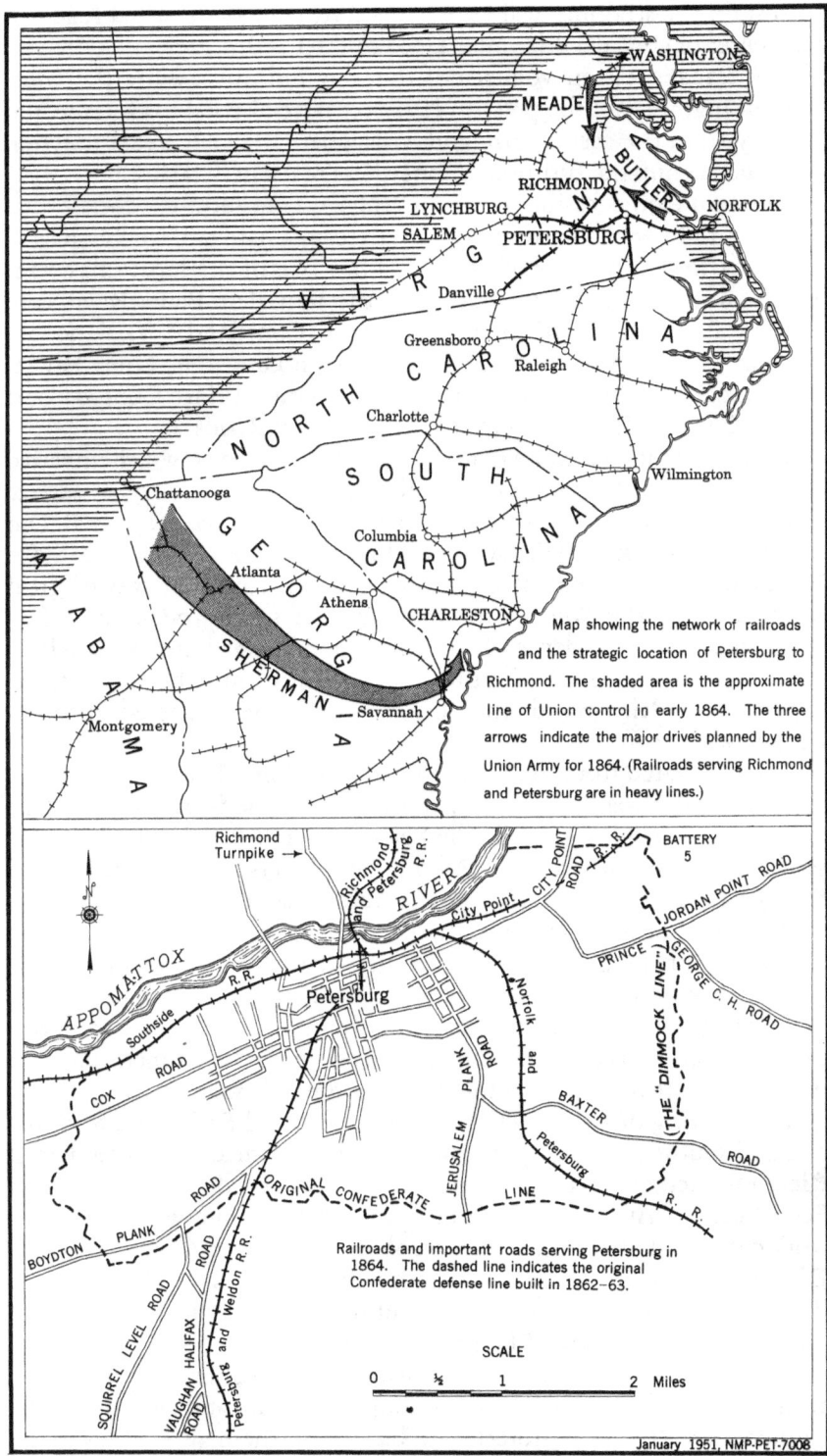

to sustain the straining war effort. In short, Petersburg was a road and rail center of considerable importance to the Confederacy.

The transportation vehicles of that day did not require the wide, straight highways of the present. However, several good roads came into the city from the east, south, and west where they effected a junction with the Richmond Turnpike. Along these roads passed supply wagons, couriers, and, on occasion, troops on their way to repel the foe. Several were built of logs laid across the road to form a hard surface. Because of this they were called "plank roads." Thus two of the most important arteries of traffic into Petersburg were the Jerusalem Plank Road, connecting Petersburg with Jerusalem (now Courtland), Va., and the Boydton Plank Road which led south through Dinwiddie Court House. Among others of importance were the City Point, Prince George Court House, Baxter, Halifax, Squirrel Level, and Cox Roads.

It was the railroads, more than the highways, however, which imparted a significance to Petersburg out of all proportion to its size. Confederate leaders were painfully aware that loss of control over their small and harassed network of railroads would mean the loss of the war. Since Petersburg was a point of convergence for five lines, it was of great importance to the South. As other lines of supply were cut off or threatened, the dependence of Richmond upon Petersburg increased. By June 1864 all but one railroad from the south into the Confederate capital—the Richmond and Danville Railroad—passed through Petersburg.

Tracks radiated from Petersburg in all directions. The Richmond and Petersburg Railroad left the city to the north. The Southside Railroad ran west to Lynchburg, while the Petersburg and Weldon Railroad led south to North Carolina. The Norfolk and Petersburg Railroad passed through a ravine east of the city before turning southeast in the direction of Norfolk. For good measure the Petersburg and City Point Railroad struck out for the hamlet of City Point, situated at the junction of the James and Appomattox Rivers 8 miles away. Because of its proximity, Petersburg was a part of the transportation system of the Confederate capital. It served as a major point of transfer to the larger metropolis for products and materials from the vast region to the south.

In the spring of 1862, McClellan had threatened Richmond from the east and southeast. This "Peninsular Campaign" made the defenders of Richmond acutely aware of the need for a system of fortifications around Petersburg. In August of that same year a defense line was begun, and work continued until its completion about a year later. Capt. Charles H. Dimmock was in charge of it under the direction of the Engineer Bureau, Confederate States Army, and the line so constructed became unofficially known as the "Dimmock Line."

When finished, the chain of breastworks and artillery emplacements around Petersburg was 10 miles long. It began and ended on the Appomattox River and protected all but the northern approaches to the city. The 55 artillery batteries were consecutively numbered from east to west. Although natural terrain features were utilized whenever possible, some glaring weaknesses existed. For example, between Batteries 7 and 8 lay a deep ravine which could provide a means of penetration by an attacking force. The very length and size of the fortifications proved to be a disadvantage. It meant that a larger number of troops would be necessary to defend the line than General Beauregard, charged with this heavy responsibility, had present for duty. Col. Alfred Roman, an aide-de-camp of Beauregard, estimated that the long "Dimmock Line" would take more than 10 times as many men to defend as were available.

The first serious threat to the untested line occurred when the Army of the James was dispatched to approach Richmond from the southeast by way of the James River. Although, the Army of the James was soon neutralized by being bottled up in Bermuda Hundred by a smaller Confederate force, it would be wrong to assume that the Union force was completely out of the picture. It not only immobilized a considerable number of Confederate soldiers assigned to guard it, but it provided a reservoir of troops for operations in other parts of the field. On several occasions raids were made on the railroads south and west of Petersburg. The most serious of these occurred on June 9, 1864, when 3,000 infantry and 1,300 cavalry appeared in force along the eastern sector of the Dimmock Line. The infantry contented itself with a menacing demonstration, but the cavalry attacked on the Jerusalem Plank Road. It was halted by the joint efforts of regular Southern Army units assisted by a hastily summoned home guard of old men and youths. The damage done by

Gen. P. G. T. Beauregard, who held the Confederate defense line before Petersburg until Lee arrived. Courtesy, National Archives.

raids such as this was quickly patched up, but they were a constant nuisance to the city's transportation lines. To shut off permanently the supplies that streamed along the railroads, the Union commanders realized that it would be necessary to take permanent physical possession of them.

The Battle of Petersburg, June 15–18, 1864

After the Battle of Cold Harbor on June 3, Grant had abandoned, for a time at least, his plan to capture Richmond by direct assault. With characteristic zeal he had ordered Meade to move the Army of the Potomac across the James River and to invest the more southerly city. On June 14 Grant and Butler conferred at Bermuda Hundred. At that time orders were given for the attack on Petersburg.

The first of the Northern forces to arrive on the scene of battle was the XVIII Corps of the Army of the James. Early in the morning of June 15 these troops, commanded by Gen. William F. Smith, crossed from Bermuda Hundred to the south side of the Appomattox by means of a pontoon bridge at Broadway Landing. Eighteen thousand Union soldiers were on their way to face less than 4,000 under Beauregard. Throughout the day they approached the city and assembled for the attack.

The Union offensive opened shortly after 7 p.m. on June 15. Among the first places to fall was Battery 5, one of the strongest of the Confederate positions. Entering the ravine between Batteries 7 and 8, Smith's men were able to approach Battery 5 and take it from the rear, the direction from which an attack was least expected. Within a few hours Beauregard had lost not only Battery 5 but all the line for more than a mile south. The defenders withdrew and threw up a hasty entrenchment along Harrison's Creek, well to the rear of the captured section of the line. While this Confederate retreat was taking place, the Union II Corps, commanded by Gen. Winfield S. Hancock, arrived to reinforce the attacking columns.

The appearance on the field of the II Corps was an ominous sign for the Confederacy. While the initial attacks were taking place on June 15, the Army of the Potomac had been busily engaged in crossing the James River farther to the east, on pontoon bridges. The number of Union troops south of the river was increasing hourly until by midnight of June 16 the entire army, numbering at least 90,000, had crossed.

Darkness ended the fighting on June 15, but early the next day the attacks were renewed. More of the defense line south of the portion captured the previous day now gave way. In response to repeated entreaties from Beauregard throughout June 15 and 16, Lee ordered more divisions to the support of Petersburg. This necessitated the draining of precious reserves from the Richmond lines. By dusk of that second day Beauregard

Broadway Landing on the Appomattox River where the XVIII Corps of the Army of the James crossed on June 15, 1864. It was later used as an ordnance depot by the Union Army. Courtesy, National Archives.

could muster about 14,000 to face the enemy. Thus, the center of attention rapidly shifted from Richmond to Petersburg, which had so recently seemed of but secondary importance.

The third day of battle was practically a repetition of that of the preceding day. Again the Northern forces attacked the Confederate troops, concentrating their efforts to the south of the positions captured earlier. Again the Confederates were forced to draw back. A decisive breakthrough of the opposing line was now anticipated by the assaulting

Pontoon bridge at Broadway Landing constructed by the Union Army in 1864. Courtesy, National Archives.

forces. At about 12:30 a. m., June 18, Beauregard ordered his troops to begin a withdrawal to new positions about a mile closer to the city. Throughout the early morning hours of that day Beauregard had his men busily engaged in the construction of this defense line. Colonel Roman, aide to Beauregard, later recalled that "without a moment's rest the digging of the trenches was begun, with such utensils as had been hastily collected at Petersburg, many of the men using their bayonets, their knives, and even their tin cans, to assist in the rapid execution of the work."

A general assault was ordered for the Union forces at 4 a. m. on June 18. When the attack began it was soon discovered that the ranks of the enemy had not been broken nor had the city fallen into Northern hands. The eastern section of the Dimmock Line was empty except for a thin line of skirmishers who were gradually forced back. The Northern troops came on, crossing the Norfolk and Petersburg Railroad south of where the defenders had constructed their line. The advance continued until they were brought face to face with the muzzles of the defender's guns. Meanwhile, elements of Lee's command continued pouring in to aid their comrades. Lee, himself, came down from his temporary headquarters near Chester, Va., to direct the defense operations in person.

Throughout that June Saturday, brisk action occurred on the new Petersburg front. The major Union drive, involving elements of four corps, came about 3 p. m. Artillery hammered the Confederates. Charges of infantry were made only to be hurled back. During the course of one of these futile drives the 1st Maine Heavy Artillery, according to William F. Fox *(Regimental Losses in the American Civil War)*, suffered the most severe losses of any regiment in a single engagement of the entire war. About 4 p. m. this unit, 850 strong, charged from the concealment of the Prince George Court House Road north of where Fort Stedman was soon to stand. Met by a heavy crossfire, it withdrew in less than one-half hour, with 632 casualties.

As on the previous days, fighting ended with the coming of darkness. Grant's attempt to capture Petersburg had failed, with a loss of 10,000 men; but his efforts could not be considered entirely unsuccessful. Two of the railroads leading into the city had been cut, and several roads were in Union hands. Behind the Northern troops was City Point which Grant speedily converted into a huge supply base.

The major result of the opening 4 days of combat, however, was the failure of the Federal forces to break the Confederate defense line. First Beauregard, and then Lee, had held against heavy odds. They had been pushed back closer to their base—but they had held. Possibly if Smith had advanced his XVIII Corps farther into the defenses on the opening night, Petersburg would have fallen on June 15 or 16. But that had not been done, and the campaign was to run nearly 10 more months.

The lines of battle before Petersburg were clearly drawn. Between 47,000 and 51,000 men defended it against 111,000 to 113,000 besiegers.

The defenses of Richmond now stretched from White Oak Swamp, east of that city, south to the Jerusalem Plank Road, 26 miles away. The fate of the Army of Northern Virginia—of the Confederate capital itself—would depend upon the outcome of the drive against Petersburg.

First Union Attempt on the Weldon Railroad

The Union Army, having failed in its initial attack on Petersburg, was now committed to doing something further to effect its capture.

The period from June 19 to July 9 was spent in three types of activity. First, elements of the army were set to work consolidating the positions captured in the 4-day battle and constructing the devices needed for siege operations. A second type of effort consisted of jabbing thrusts at the important supply routes into Petersburg. The last was a reconnoitering of the Confederate defenses to determine a plan which would result in the fall of the city.

A threatening movement toward the Weldon Railroad was soon made by the Northern troops. Three days after the failure to capture the city a small force began to push to the southwest of Grant's flank on the Jerusalem Plank Road. The following day, June 22, Confederate divisions led by Generals Cadmus M. Wilcox and William Mahone advanced from the defense line south of Petersburg and forced the Union troops to a temporary halt.

The next morning saw the resumption of the advance toward the Weldon Railroad. A small cavalry force was successful in reaching the tracks on the 23d, and it promptly started the work of destruction which was its mission. Alarmed by the threat to this important supply line, the Confederates launched a sharp attack which forced the withdrawal of the Union forces from the vicinity of the railroad. However, the Union lines confronting Petersburg had been extended across the Jerusalem Plank Road, thus cutting off its use to the city.

In itself the battle of June 22–23 was not important. The North could quickly replace the loss of 2,300 men. The railroad, although its days were numbered, was still able to deliver a few supplies to Petersburg. But as an indication of Grant's tactics, it pointed the course of the campaign ahead. It marked the first of several attempts to encircle Petersburg. The others to follow would not all be as disappointing to Northern hopes. In these repeated drives to the west lay the essence of the basic tactics to capture Petersburg.

On July 9, 1864, the plan of operations decided upon by the Union high command was revealed in an order issued from Meade's headquarters. This order gave detailed instructions on the building of fortifications and the development of siege tactics. Thus it became apparent that the Union plan was to reduce Petersburg by a lengthy process of attrition.

Lt. Col. Henry Pleasants, Commanding Officer of the 48th Pennsylvania Infantry Regiment which dug the Union tunnel under the Confederate line. From Battles and Leaders of the Civil War.

There were still those in the attacking forces, however, who felt that, with a little imagination, the city could be taken by direct assault. While most of the troops were digging siege lines, another, and smaller, group had already begun work on a unique plan which would, if successful, make further encirclement unnecessary.

The Battle of the Crater, July 30, 1864

At several places east of the city the opposing lines were extremely close together. One of these locations was in front of Elliott's Salient, a Confederate strong point near Cemetery Hill and old Blandford Church. Here the Confederate position and the Union picket line were less than 400 feet apart. Because of the proximity of the Union line, Elliott's Salient was well fortified. Behind earthen embankments was a battery of four guns, and two veteran South Carolina infantry regiments were stationed on either side. Behind these were other defensive works; before them the ground sloped gently downward toward the Union advance line.

This forward Union line was built on the crest of a ravine which had been crossed on June 18. Through this ravine, and between the sentry line and the main line, lay the roadbed of the Norfolk and Petersburg Railroad. The front in this sector was manned by Gen. Ambrose E. Burnside's IX Corps. Among the many units which composed this corps was the 48th Regiment, Pennsylvania Veteran Volunteer Infantry. A large

Cross-section view of a scale model of the Union tunnel.

The explosion of the Union mine as recorded by A. R. Waud, a

contemporary artist. From Battles and Leaders of the Civil War.

proportion of this regiment had been coal miners, and it seemed to have occurred to one or more of them that Elliott's Salient would provide an excellent place to use their civilian occupation. Lt. Col. Henry Pleasants, the commanding officer of the 48th and a mining engineer by profession, overheard one of the enlisted men mutter, "We could blow that damned fort out of existence if we could run a mine shaft under it." From this and similar remarks came the germ of the idea for the Union mine. This is what the 48th Regiment proposed to do: dig a long gallery from the bottom of the ravine behind their picket line to a point beneath the Confederate battery at Elliott's Salient, blow up the position by means of powder placed in the end of the tunnel, and, finally, send a strong body of troops through the gap created in the enemy's line by the explosion. They saw as the reward for their effort the capitulation of Petersburg and, perhaps, the end of the war.

After obtaining the permission of Burnside and Grant, Pleasants and his men commenced digging their mine shaft on June 25. The lack of proper equipment made it necessary constantly to improvise tools and apparatus with which to excavate. Mining picks were created from straightened army picks. Cracker boxes were converted into handbarrows in which the dirt was removed from the end of the tunnel. A sawmill changed a bridge into timber necessary for shoring up the mine. Pleasants estimated both direction and depth of the tunnel by means of a theodolite (old-fashioned even in 1864) sent him from Washington. The outmoded instrument served its purpose well, however; the mine shaft hit exactly beneath the salient at which it was aimed.

One of the most remarkable features of the gallery was the method devised to supply the diggers at the end with fresh air. The longer the tunnel grew, the more serious became the problem of ventilation. It had been considered impossible to dig a tunnel for any considerable distance without spacing shafts at regular intervals in order to replace the polluted air with a fresh supply. This problem had been solved by the application of the simple physical principle that warm air tends to rise. Behind the Union picket line and to the right of the mine gallery, although connected with it, the miners dug a ventilating chimney. Between the chimney and the mine entrance they erected an airtight canvas door. Through that door and along the floor of the gallery there was laid a square wooden pipe. A fire was then built at the bottom of the ventilating shaft. As the fire warmed the air it went up the chimney. The draft thus created drew the bad air from the end of the tunnel where the men were digging. As this went out, fresh air was drawn in through the wooden pipe to replace it.

Work on the tunnel had been continuously pushed from the start on June 25. By July 17 the diggers were nearly 511 feet from the entrance and directly beneath the battery in Elliott's Salient. The Confederates had become suspicious by this time, for the faint sounds of digging could be heard issuing from the earth. Their apprehension took the form of countermines behind their own lines. Several of these were dug in an effort to locate the Union gallery. Two were very close, being sunk on either side of where the Pennsylvanians were at work. Although digging in the countermines continued throughout the month of July, Confederate fears seemed to quiet down during the same period. There were many reasons for this. One was the failure of their tunnels to strike any Union construction. Another major reason, undoubtedly, was a belief held by many that it was impossible to ventilate a shaft of any length over 400 feet without constructing air shafts along it.

The next step in the Union plan was to burrow out into lateral galleries at the end of the long shaft. Accordingly, on July 18 work was begun on these branches which extended to the right and left, paralleling the Confederate fortifications above. When completed, these added another 75 feet to the total length of the tunnel which now reached 586 feet into the earth. It was about 20 feet from the floor of the tunnel to the enemy works above. The average internal dimensions of the shaft were 5 feet high, with a base 4½ feet in width tapering to 2 feet at the top.

Digging was finally completed on July 23. Four days later the task of charging the mine with black powder was accomplished. Three hundred and twenty kegs of powder weighing, on the average, 25 pounds each were arranged in the two lateral galleries in eight magazines. The total charge was 4 tons, or 8,000 pounds. The powder was sandbagged to direct the force of the explosion upward and two fuses were spliced together to form a 98-foot line.

Meanwhile, preparations for the attack which was to follow the explosion of the mine had been carried out. Burnside was convinced of the necessity for a large-scale attack by the entire IX Corps. His request was acceded to by Meade and Grant with but one important exception. It had been Burnside's hope that a fresh and numerically strong (about 4,300) Negro division should lead the charge after the explosion. Meade opposed this on the grounds that if the attack failed the Union commanders could be accused of wanting to get rid of the only Negro troops then with the Army of the Potomac. Burnside was not informed of this decision until the day before the battle, July 29, and he was forced to change his plans at the last moment. Three white divisions were to make the initial charge along with the colored troops. Burnside had the commanding generals of these three divisions draw straws to see which would lead. Gen. James F. Ledlie of the 1st Division won the draw.

Despite these eleventh-hour changes, a plan of battle had been evolved. During the night of July 29–30 the bulk of the IX Corps had assembled in the ravine behind the mine entrance. Troops from other Union corps were sent to act as reinforcements. A total of 110 guns and 54 mortars was alerted to begin their shelling of the Confederate line. A Union demonstration before Richmond had forced Lee to withdraw troops from Petersburg. Only about 18,000 soldiers were left to guard the city.

A contemporary sketch by Waud showing the Union charge to

the Crater. From Battles and Leaders of the Civil War.

At 3:15 a. m., July 30, Pleasants lit the fuse of the mine and mounted the parapet to see the results of his regiment's work. The explosion was expected at 3:30 a. m. Minutes passed slowly by, and the men huddled behind the lines grew more apprehensive. By 4:15 there could be no doubt but that something had gone wrong. Two volunteers from the 48th Regiment (Lt. Jacob Douty and Sgt. Harry Reese) crawled into the tunnel and found that the fuse had burned out at the splice. They relighted it and scrambled to safety. Finally, at about 4:45 a. m., the explosion took place. The earth trembled as men, equipment, and debris were hurled high into the air. At least 278 Confederate troops were killed or wounded in the tremendous blast, and 2 of the 4 guns in the battery were destroyed beyond repair. The measurements of the size of the crater torn by the powder vary considerably, but it seems to have been at least 170 feet long, 60 to 80 feet wide, and 30 feet deep.

The awesome spectacle of the mine explosion caused a delay in the Union charge following the explosion. Removal of obstructions between the lines caused further delay. Soon, however, an advance was made to the crater where many of the attacking force paused to seek shelter on its steep slopes or to look at the havoc caused by the mine. The hard-pressed Confederates rallied quickly and soon were pouring shells and bullets into their opponents. Union reinforcements poured into the breach; but, instead of going forward, they either joined their comrades

The Crater as it appeared in 1865. The Union soldier seated at the end of the tunnel gives an idea of the size of the Crater. Courtesy, National Archives.

in the crater or branched out to the immediate right and left along the lines. By 8:30 that morning a large part of the IX Corps had been poured into the captured enemy salient. Over 15,000 troops now filled and surrounded the crater.

By prompt action and determined effort the Confederates had stopped the attack. The attention of three batteries was soon directed on the Blue-clad men in the crater. Repeated volleys of artillery shot and shell raked the huddled groups of increasingly demoralized men. In addition, mortars were brought to within 50 yards of the crater and started to drop shells on the soldiers with deadly effect.

Successful as these devices were in halting the Union advance, Lee was aware that an infantry charge would be necessary to dislodge the enemy. By 6 a. m. an order had been sent to General Mahone to move two brigades of his division from the lines south of Petersburg to the defense of the threatened position. Then Lee joined Beauregard in observing the battle from the Gee house, 500 yards to the rear of the scene of strife.

In spite of the Confederate resistance, most of the Northern Negro division and other regiments had, by 8 a. m., advanced a short distance beyond their companions at the crater. Shortly after 8 o'clock Mahone's Confederate division began to arrive on the scene. The men filed into a ravine about 200 yards west of the crater and between it and Petersburg. No sooner had they entered this protected position than, perceiving the danger to their lines, they charged across the open field into the mass of enemy soldiers. Although outnumbered, they forced the Northerners to flee back to the comparative shelter of the crater. Then they swept

Maj. Gen. William Mahone, Confederate leader at the Battle of the Crater. Courtesy, National Archives.

on to regain a portion of the line north of the Union-held position.

Again, at about 10:30 a. m., more of Mahone's troops charged, but were repulsed. Meanwhile, the lot of the Northern soldiers was rapidly becoming unbearable. The spectacle within the crater was appalling. Confederate artillery continued to beat upon them. The closely packed troops (dead, dying, and living mixed indiscriminately together) lacked shade from the blazing sun, food, water and, above all, competent leadership. Meade had ordered their withdrawal more than an hour before the second Confederate charge, but Burnside delayed the transmission of the order till after midday. Many men had chosen to run the gantlet of fire back to their own lines, but others remained clinging to the protective sides of the crater.

The last scene in the battle occurred shortly after 1 p. m. A final charge by Mahone's men was successful in gaining the slopes of the crater. Some of the Union men, overcome with exhaustion and realizing the helplessness of their situation, surrendered; but others continued to fight. At one point where resistance centered, the Confederates put their hats on ramrods and lifted them over the rim of the crater. The caps were promptly torn to shreds by a volley. Before their foe could reload, Mahone's forces jumped into the crater where a desperate struggle with bayonets, rifle butts, and fists ensued.

Soon it was all over. The Union Army had suffered a loss of over 4,000 in killed, wounded, or captured as against about 1,500 for the Confederates. Again, as on June 15–18, a frontal assault had failed to take the Confederate citadel.

The Fight for the Weldon Railroad

Grant, if he reviewed the fruits of his campaign shortly after July 30, could not have felt much comfort. Two hammering blows delivered against Petersburg had failed. Moreover, two important railroads still connected the city with the south. Lee, despite his numerically inferior numbers, was still able to maintain a long line of defenses around Petersburg and Richmond. Farther south, the Union outlook was brighter. Two days before the Battle of the Crater, final operations against Atlanta had been begun by Sherman. On September 2 it was to fall and the march to the sea follow.

Yet it was equally certain that Grant had accomplished an important objective. By committing Lee's weakened but still potent Army of Northern Virginia to a defensive position in the area adjacent to the Capital he was immobilizing the South's most powerful striking force. Moreover, the Union failure at the crater decided the future direction of the campaign to capture Petersburg. All Grant's energy now turned to extending siege fortifications around the city.

The first step taken in this direction after July 30 was a strong effort to capture the Weldon Railroad, which the Confederates had so nearly lost in June. On August 16, Gen. Gouverneur K. Warren, Union V Corps commander, received orders to attack, occupy, and hold the Weldon Railroad 3 miles below the city.

The seizure of the objective was quickly accomplished on August 18, the opening day of battle. More than a mile of track in the vicinity of an old colonial inn named Globe Tavern was soon in Union hands. Then Warren marched most of his forces northward toward the city. Soon they were in unfamiliar and heavily wooded terrain where they encountered strong artillery and musket fire from the enemy. They then halted and bivouacked in the woods below Petersburg.

On the afternoon of the next day, August 19, four brigades of Gen. A. P. Hill's Corps struck the Union infantry. Two of the brigades managed to slip in behind their opponents by taking advantage of the concealment offered by the heavy growth of trees. They inflicted serious losses and captured 2,700 prisoners. By nightfall Warren had been forced back a half mile nearer his new headquarters at Globe Tavern.

August 20 was marked by comparative inactivity, although there was some skirmishing in the morning. Throughout the following day Hill threw his men at the Union positions around the tavern. The attacks were in vain, for the new Union lines held. General Lee arrived with infantry replacements during the afternoon, but even this did not turn the tide of battle. By the end of the day Lee realized that the upper portion of the Weldon Railroad had been lost and that any attempt to regain it would be a needless sacrifice of manpower.

One sentence from a dispatch sent by Lee to the Confederate Secretary of War on August 22 shows the seriousness of the loss of the railroad:

Globe Tavern near the Weldon Railroad. This building served as headquarters for the Union V Corps (Maj. Gen. G. K. Warren) during the Battle of Globe Tavern, August 18–21, 1864. Courtesy, National Archives.

Union soldier on picket duty in the lines before Petersburg. Courtesy, National Archives.

"Our supply of corn is exhausted today, and I am informed that the small reserve in Richmond is consumed." For a time the Confederate government was able to utilize the Weldon Railroad as far as Stony Creek, 20 miles below Petersburg, where supplies were transferred to wagons and hauled around the left of the Northern Army to Petersburg and Richmond. Soon the railroad line was destroyed below Stony Creek and henceforth the beleaguered cities had only two direct rail communications with the south. These were the Richmond and Danville Railroad out of Richmond and the Southside from Petersburg.

On August 25, 4 days after the attack on Globe Tavern, the Confederates scored a minor victory with a surprise attack. Their blow was aimed at the Union II Corps which was engaged in destroying railroad tracks at Reams Station, nearly 5 miles below Globe Tavern. The II Corps, containing large numbers of inexperienced recruits, was badly beaten and more than 2,000 were taken prisoner. The Southern victory was short-lived, for the destruction of their rail communications was continued. The best that Lee could hope for in the future would be to stem the Blue advance.

In mid-September, Wade Hampton, cavalry commander of the Army of Northern Virginia, led a remarkable raid of 4,000 mounted troops around the rear of the Union Army, which now numbered 80,000. He succeeded in returning to Petersburg on September 17 with over 2,400 head of cattle and more than 300 prisoners, while suffering losses of only 61 men in two engagements with the enemy. Although this raised the morale of the Confederates, it did not change the course of the campaign. The iron band being forged outside their city was a reality, and Grant, a tenacious man, had not loosened his grip.

The wharves and supply vessels at City Point, Va., Union headquarters and supply base on the James River. Courtesy, National Archives.

Union Encirclement Continues

The relentless westerly advance of the besieging force was soon resumed after the capture of the Weldon Railroad in August. Constant skirmishing occurred between the lines until, in late September, Grant struck again.

The Battle of Peebles' Farm, September 29 to October 1, was really the second section of a two-part struggle. The first took place closer to Richmond and was directed at Fort Harrison, a strongly fortified point on the outer defense line of the capital. Fort Harrison was located a mile north of the James River and approximately midway between Richmond and Petersburg. On the morning of September 29, Union troops advanced and captured the fort and held it the next day against a counterattack by the late occupants. At the same time Meade was moving toward a further encirclement of Petersburg with about 16,000 troops. The direction of his attack was northwest toward Confederate earthworks along the Squirrel Level Road. The ultimate goal was the capture of the Southside Railroad.

Fighting began on the 29th as the Blue vanguard approached the Confederates in the vicinity of Peebles' Farm. The engagement increased in fury on the 30th and continued into the 1st day of October. When the smoke of battle had blown away on October 2, Meade had extended the Union left flank 3 miles farther west and had secured the ground on which Fort Fisher would soon be built. This fort was to be the Union's biggest and was one of the largest earthen forts in Civil War history. He had, however, stopped short of the coveted Southside Railroad. Against the gain in territory the Union Army had suffered a loss of over 1,500

25

Please refer to your Official Park Map for a current list of tour stops.
This is a depiction of the Park in 1951.

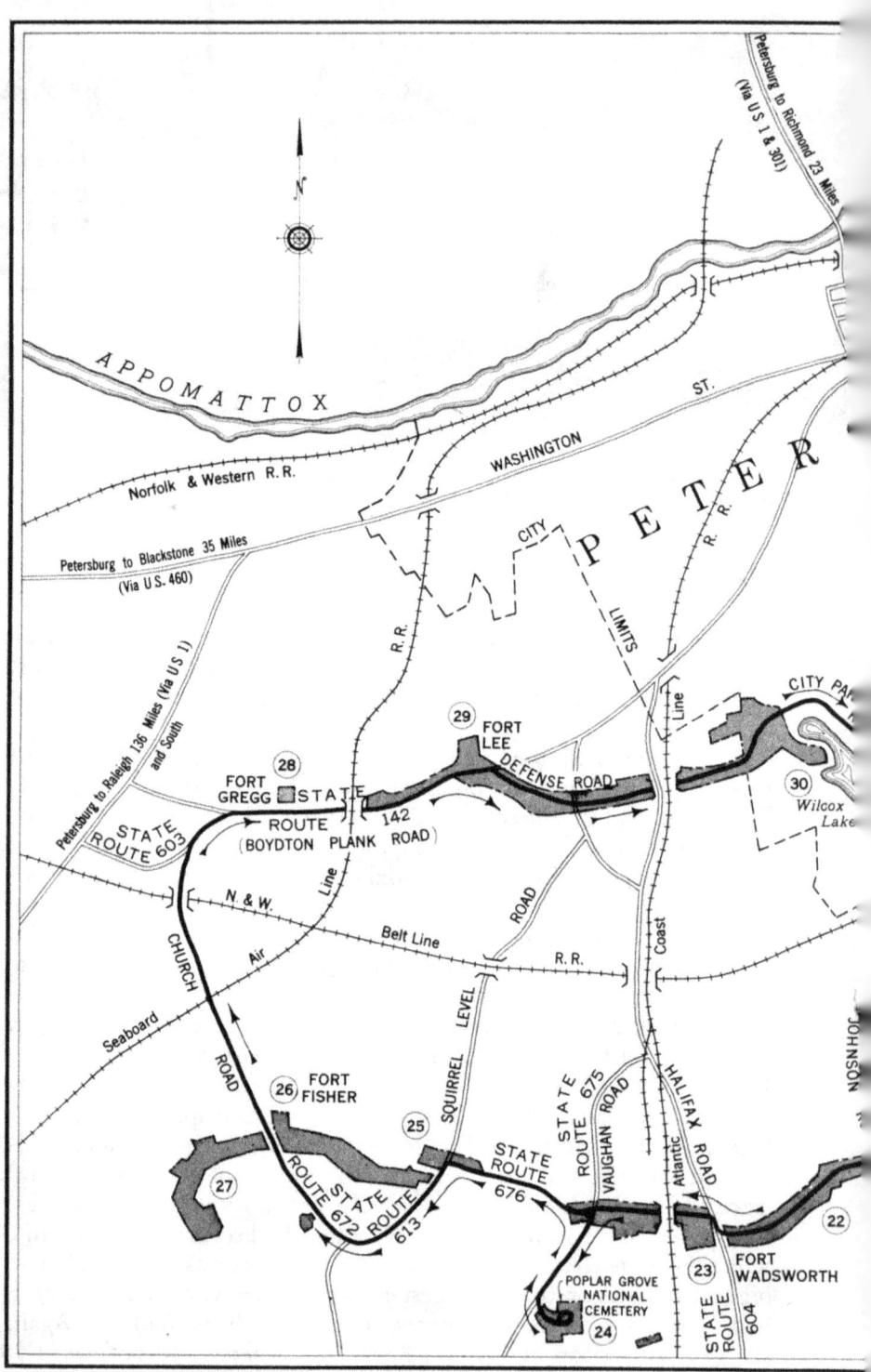

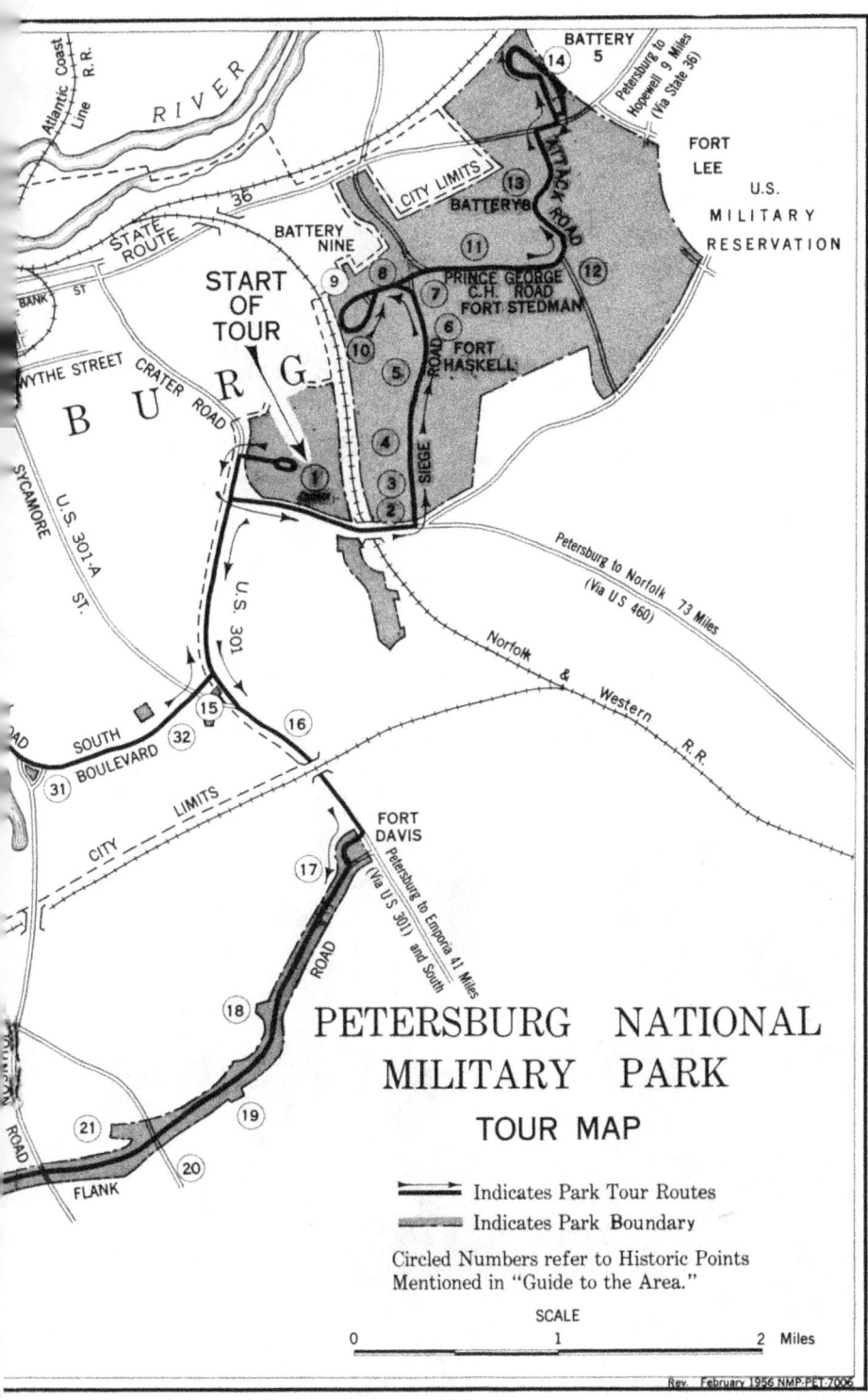

Photograph of one of the engines used on the United States military railroad taken at City Point in 1865. This engine hauled men and supplies to various parts of the long line around Petersburg. Courtesy, National Archives.

"The Dictator" or "The Petersburg Express," a 13-inch, 17,000-pound mortar which the Union Army used to shell Petersburg from a distance of two and one-half miles. Courtesy, National Archives.

prisoners to the Confederacy and more than 1,000 in killed and wounded. The Southerners found that their lines, while unbroken, were again extended. Each extension meant a thinner Confederate defense line.

For a period of a little over 3 weeks after the Battle of Peebles' Farm the shovel and pick again replaced the musket as the principal tools for soldiers on both sides. Forts were built, breastworks dug, and gabions constructed. Then, on October 27, the Union troops moved again. This time they turned toward Boydton Plank Road and a stream known as Hatcher's Run, 12 miles southwest of Petersburg.

The general plan of operations was nearly the same as that used at Peebles' Farm. Butler's Army of the James was ordered to threaten attack in front of Richmond. Meanwhile, at the left of the Union line 17,000 infantry and cavalry of the Army of the Potomac started for the Boydton Plank Road. They made rapid progress, driving the enemy outposts ahead of them and advancing in two long columns until they reached the vicinity of Burgess' Mill where the Boydton Plank Road crossed Hatcher's Run.

It was in the neighborhood of Burgess' Mill that heavy Confederate opposition was met. Here a spirited engagement took place between the two contending forces. A failure of Union Generals Hancock of the II Corps and Warren of the V Corps to coordinate the efforts of their respective columns, coupled with stout Confederate infantry resistance and a dashing charge by Hampton's cavalry in a manner reminiscent of "Jeb" Stuart, resulted in a speedy Northern withdrawal. The Boydton Plank Road, for a time at least, remained in Southern hands, and Grant's encircling movement had received a temporary check.

The approach of winter made any large-scale effort by either side less probable, although daily skirmishes and tightening of the siege lines continued. The slackening of hostile action was used to good advantage by Union and Confederate alike, as it had been in the previous respites between battles, in the strengthening of the battle lines and efforts to develop some rudimentary comforts in the cheerless camps. Throughout the last 2 months of 1864 and the first month of the new year there were no strong efforts by either side before Petersburg; picket duty, sniping, and patrolling prevailed. Lee now had a 35-mile front, with the left resting on the Williamsburg Road east of Richmond and the right on Hatcher's Run southwest of Petersburg. To hold this long line he had but 57,402 effective soldiers on December 31. Facing these undernourished and ragged soldiers, there were, according to official returns of the same date, 110,364 well-fed and equipped Union troops.

The picture throughout the rest of the South was no more reassuring to the Confederate sympathizers. In the Shenandoah Valley of Virginia, northwest of Richmond, Gen. Philip H. Sheridan had crushed the Southern forces of Gen. Jubal A. Early at Cedar Creek on October 19 and was destroying the scattered resistance that remained. Far to the south Gen. William T. Sherman had captured Atlanta, Ga., in September 1864,

A section of the Union siege line around Petersburg. Note the use of wickerware (gabions), sharpened stakes (fraises), and branches (abatis) to protect the lines. Courtesy, National Archives.

Making sap rollers, Union line. Courtesy, National Archives

Deserted huts on the Confederate line in 1865. Courtesy, National Archives.

and Savannah had surrendered on December 21. As the new year dawned, his army was prepared to march north toward Grant. To complete the gloomy Southern prospects, Fort Fisher, bastion of Wilmington, N. C., which was the last of the great Atlantic Coast ports to remain in their possession, was under fatal bombardment by mid-January.

The Battle of Hatcher's Run, February 5 to 7, 1865, was the result of a further drive by the Northern forces in their attempt to encircle Petersburg. The two Union Corps (the II and the V), which had been stopped at Burgess' Mill, again marched toward Hatcher's Run. As before, their objective was the Boydton Plank Road. This time they reached their goal with little trouble on February 5.

Union battery of Parrott guns before Petersburg. Courtesy, National Archives.

Camp scene on the Union line. Behind the seated soldiers are good examples of the type of improvised quarters built by many of the troops. Courtesy, National Archives.

Confederate opposition to this advance lasted through 3 days, but it was ineffective. This was due to several factors: the inferior numbers of the Southern Army, the extremely bad weather which made a Union attack appear unlikely, the ravages of cold on badly equipped and uniformed men, and, most important, the breakdown of the food supply system.

After having been successful in capturing the Boydton Plank Road and beating off Confederate attacks, the Northern leaders decided that the road was not worth holding. It was not as important an artery of traffic as they had supposed. Consequently, they made no attempt to hold it, but they did occupy and fortify the newly extended line to Hatcher's Run at a point 3 miles below Burgess' Mill. Thus, again the Union lines had been pushed to the west, and, as before, Lee was forced to lengthen his defenses. The Petersburg-Richmond front with its recent extension now stretched over 37 miles, and the army holding it had dwindled through casualties and desertion to a little more than 46,000 in number on March 1, 1865.

The Battle of Hatcher's Run was another fight in the constant movement of the Union Army to the west after June 18, 1864. In its relentless extension around Petersburg, which continued day by day with the addition of a few more feet or yards of picket line and rifle pits, there had occurred five important thrusts aimed by the Northern leaders at encir-

Maj. Gen. John B. Gordon, Confederate commander at the Battle of Fort Stedman. Courtesy, National Archives.

cling Petersburg. They included two attacks on the Weldon Railroad, in June and August 1864; Peebles' Farm, in September and October; Burgess' Mill, in October; and, finally, the move on the Boydton Plank Road in February 1865. They met with varying degrees of success, but still the Union noose was not drawn tightly enough.

The enlisted men of both armies, however, remained largely unaware of the strategy of their commanders. Their daily existence during the campaign took on a marked flavor, different in many respects from the more dashing engagements which preceded it. Too often war is a combination of bloodshed and boredom, and Petersburg, unlike most other military operations of the Civil War, had more than its share of the latter. The Petersburg episode—assault and resistance—dragged on to become the longest unbroken campaign against a single city in the history of the United States. The romantic and heroic exploits were relatively few, and between them came long stretches of uninspiring and backbreaking routine.

The men of both sides had much in common, despite the bitterness with which they fought. In battle they were enemies, but in camp they were on the same common level. Stripped of the emotional tension and exhilaration of combat they all appear as bored, war-weary, homesick men. The greater part of their time was primarily concerned with digging and constructing fortifications, performing sentry and picket duty, and striving to speed up the long succession of days. They lived in rude improvised shelters, often made of mud and log walls with tent roofs.

Chimneys were made of mud and barrels. There was some friendly interchange of words and gifts between the lines, but enmity was more rampant than brotherly regard. Off duty, the amusements and pastimes of the soldiers were simple and few—limited in most cases to their ability to improvise them. The most striking difference between the armies as the Petersburg campaign lengthened was that, while the Northerners suffered most from boredom, the Confederates were plagued by the more serious and unpleasant pangs of hunger.

The Petersburg campaign, however, was grim business. Amusements could lighten the heart for only a brief time at best. Ever present were the mud and disease which followed every Civil War camp. Both opposing forces felt the chill of winter and the penetrating rain. The discouragement of the homesick, who never knew when, or if, he would return to his fireside, was not a hardship peculiar to any rank. However, when spring came to warm the air there was a difference between the two armies. It was more than a numerical superiority. Then the Union trooper felt confidence, while the Southern veteran, ill-clothed, ill-fed, and nearly surrounded, knew only despair.

The South Strikes Back—The Battle of Fort Stedman

By mid-March of 1865 the climax of the campaign, and of the war, was close at hand. Lee's forces in both Richmond and Petersburg had dwindled to under 50,000, with only 35,000 fit for duty. Grant, on the other hand, had available, or within easy march, at least 150,000. Moreover, Sheridan, having destroyed the remnants of Early's forces at Waynesboro, Va., on March 2, had cleared the Shenandoah Valley of Confederates and was now free to join Grant before Petersburg.

Everywhere Lee turned the picture was black. Union forces under Sherman, driving Johnston before them, split the Confederacy and were now in North Carolina. With President Jefferson Davis' consent, Lee sent a letter to General Grant on March 2 suggesting an interview. In the early morning hours of the second day following the dispatch of the letter, Lee and Maj. Gen. John B. Gordon discussed the three possible solutions to the problem which perplexed them. In order, they were as follows:

(1) Try to negotiate satisfactory peace terms. This had already been acted upon in Lee's note to Grant.
(2) Retreat from Richmond and Petersburg and unite with Johnston for a final stand.
(3) Attack Grant in order to facilitate the retreat.

There followed a series of interviews with high Government officials in Richmond. Each of the plans was analyzed. The first was quickly dropped when Grant made it clear that he was not empowered to nego-

An exterior view of Fort Stedman as it appeared in 1865.
Courtesy, National Archives.

tiate. Nor was the second proposal, that of retreat, deemed advisable by President Davis who wished to strike one more blow before surrendering his capital. This left only the third alternative—to attack.

The plan evolved by the Southern commander was relatively simple. He ordered General Gordon to make a reconnaissance of the lines around Petersburg. Gordon soon reported that the best place for the proposed attack was at Fort Stedman. This Union position was near the City Point Railroad which Grant used as a major supply line between his base at City Point and the entrenchments around Petersburg. Capture of this railroad would cut the Northern supply line. An additional advantage, from the Confederate viewpoint, was the fact that Fort Stedman was but 150 yards to the east of a strongly fortified Southern position named Colquitt's Salient.

About one-half of the besieged army would be used to charge the Union line in the vicinity of Fort Stedman. It was hoped that this would cause Grant to shorten his front in order to protect the endangered supply route. Then Lee could detach a portion of his army to send to the aid of Johnston as, with shorter lines, he would not need as many men in Petersburg. Should the attack fail, he would attempt to retreat with his forces intact for a final stand with Johnston. This was the last desperate gamble of the Army of Northern Virginia.

The details for the attack were worked out by Gordon. During the night preceding the attack, the obstructions before the Confederate lines were to be removed and the Union pickets overcome as quietly as possible. A group of 50 men were to remove the chevaux-de-frise and abatis protecting Fort Stedman; then 3 companies of 100 men each were to charge and capture the fort. When Stedman was safely in Confederate hands, these men were to pretend they were Union troops and, forming into 3 columns, were to rush to the rear to capture other positions.

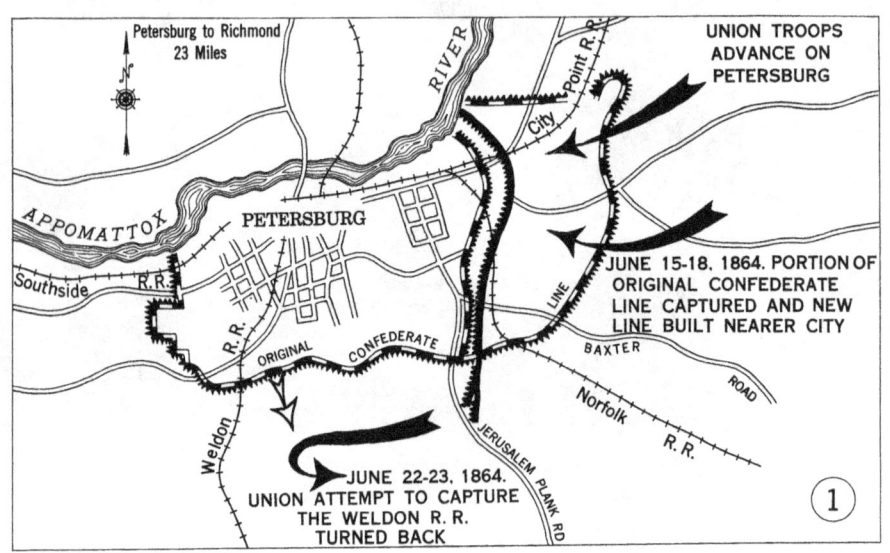

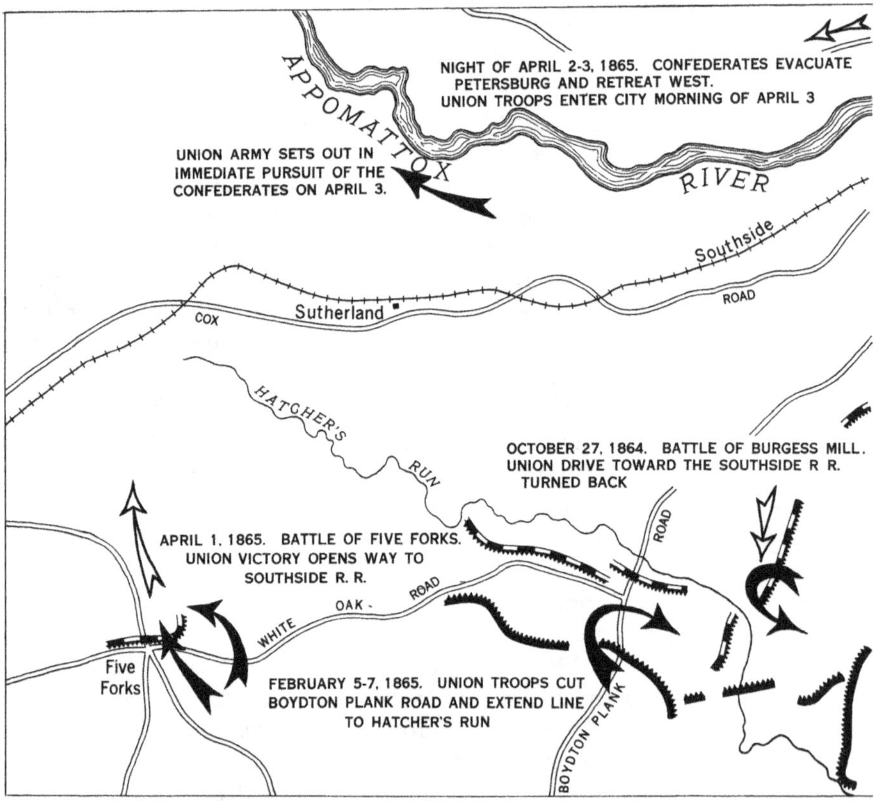

THE PETERSBURG CAMPAIGN

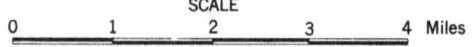

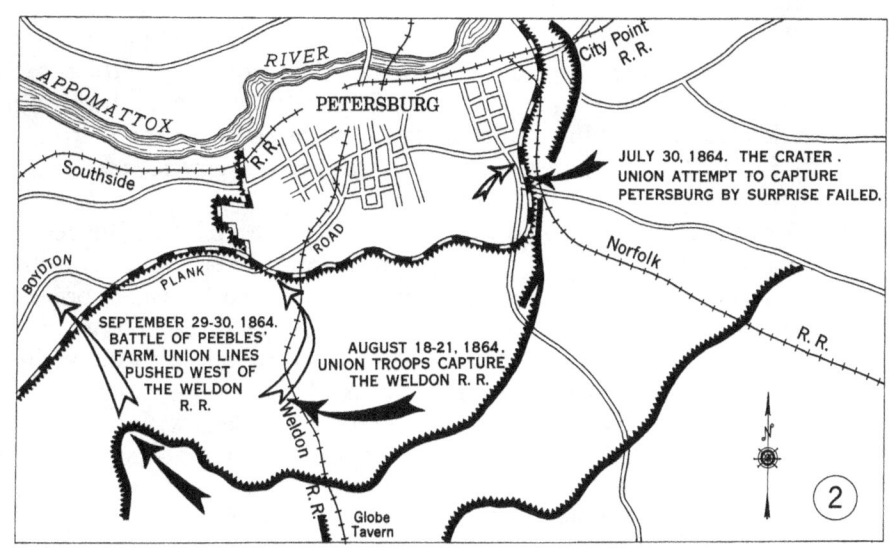

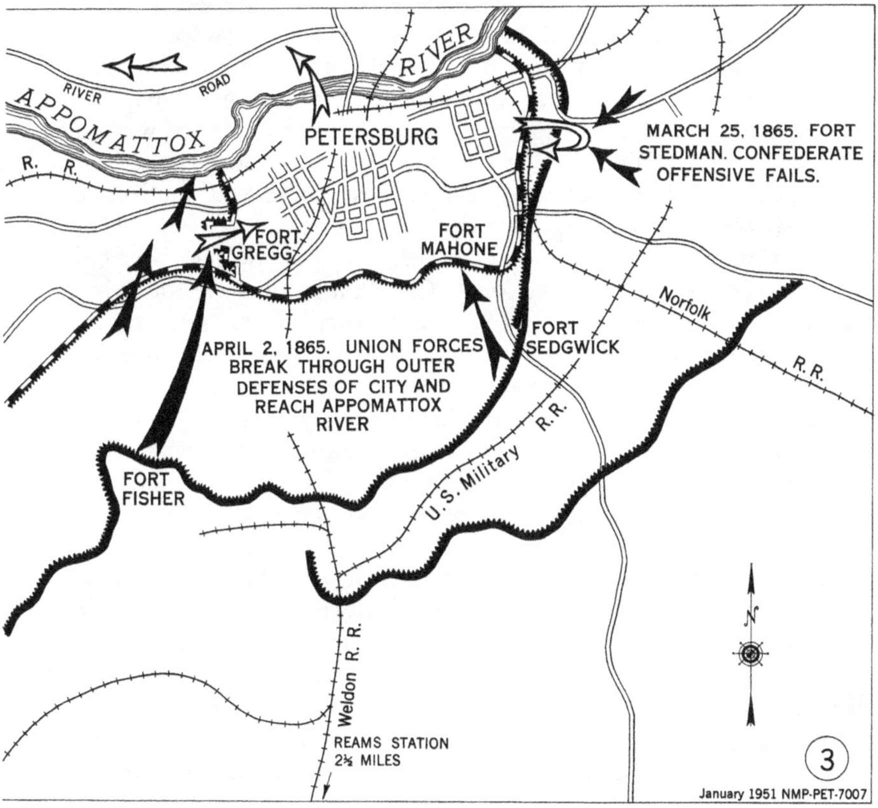

The next step was to send a division of infantry to gain possession of the siege lines north and south of the fallen bastion. When the breach had been sufficiently widened, Southern cavalry were to rush through and destroy telegraphic communication with Grant's headquarters at City Point. They were also ordered to cut the military railroad. Additional reserves were to follow the cavalry.

The attack was scheduled for the morning of March 25. The 50 axemen and the 300 soldiers who were to make up the advance columns were given strips of white cloth to wear across their breasts in order to tell friend from foe. The officers in charge were given the names of Union officers known to be in the vicinity and were told to shout their assumed names if challenged. Beginning about 3 a. m., Confederates professing to be deserters crossed to the Union pickets with requests to surrender. Their actual purpose was to be near at hand to overwhelm the unsuspecting pickets when the attack began.

At 4 a. m. Gordon gave the signal, and the Confederates sprang forward. At first the attack went as planned. Blue-clad pickets were silenced so effectively that not a shot was fired. Union obstructions were quickly hewn down by the axemen, and the small vanguard of 300 swept through Battery 10 which stood immediately north of Fort Stedman. They then rushed into the fort from the northwest. The sleeping, or partially awakened, occupants were completely surprised and surrendered without a fight. Battery 11 to the south of Fort Stedman was also soon in Confederate hands. Union resistance in this early stage was ineffective, although Battery 11 was recaptured for a brief time.

More Confederates pressed into the torn line. While the three columns set out in the general direction of City Point and along the Prince George Court House Road behind Stedman, other infantry units moved north and south along the Federal emplacements. To the north they captured the fortifications as far as Battery 9 where they were stopped by the Union defenders. In the opposite direction they progressed as far as the ramparts of Fort Haskell. A desperate struggle ensued, but here, too, the Northerners refused to yield. Despite these checks, the Confederates were now in possession of about three-fourths of a mile of the Union line.

In the center of the Confederate attack the three small columns quickly advanced as far as Harrison's Creek—a small stream which winds its way north to the Appomattox River 650 yards behind Fort Stedman. One of the columns succeeded in crossing the stream and continuing toward a small Union artillery post on the site of what had been Confederate Battery 8, but canister from the post forced the column back to the creek. Confusion took hold of the Confederates who were unable to locate the positions they had been ordered to capture in the rear of the Union line. Artillery fire from Northern guns on a ridge to the east held them on the banks of Harrison's Creek. By 6 a. m. their forward momentum had been checked.

Union infantry then charged from the ridge to attack the Southerners. The forces joined battle along the banks of Harrison's Creek and the Confederates were soon forced back to Fort Stedman. For a brief time they held their newly captured positions. At 7:30 a. m. Gen. John F. Hartranft advanced on them with a division of Northern troops. Heavy musket and artillery fire on Gordon's men threatened them with annihilation unless they retired to their own lines soon. Shortly after 7:30 a. m., Gordon received an order from Lee to withdraw his men. The order was quickly dispatched across the open fields to the soldiers in the captured Union works. By now, however, the line of retreat was raked by a vicious crossfire and many Confederates preferred surrender to withdrawal. About 7:45 a. m., the Union line was completely restored and the forlorn Southern hope of a successful disruption of Northern communications, followed by secret withdrawal from the city, was now lost. Equally bad, if not worse, to the Confederates was the loss of more than 4,000 killed, wounded, and captured as compared to the Union casualties of less than 1,500.

Of the three Confederate plans of action before the Battle of Fort Stedman, now only the second—retreat—was possible. The situation demanded immediate action, for, even as Gordon had been preparing on March 24 to launch his attack, Grant had been engaged in planning more difficulties for the harassed defenders of Petersburg.

Union Encirclement Becomes a Reality

The coming of better weather heralded the opportunity for the final blows against the city. Grant, who was now passing some of the most anxious moments of his life, planned that this effort should be concentrated on the extreme right of the long Confederate line which protected Richmond and Petersburg. This meant that hostilities would soon commence somewhere west of Hatcher's Run, perhaps in the neighborhood of Dinwiddie Court House or a road junction called Five Forks which lay 17 miles southwest of Petersburg. On March 24, Grant ordered the II and IX Corps and three divisions of the Army of the James to the extreme left of the Union lines facing Lee. This resulted in a strong concentration southwest of Hatcher's Run. Two days later Gen. Philip Sheridan arrived in City Point, fresh from a victorious campaign in the Shenandoah Valley, and was ordered to join his troops to the concentration on the left. Finally, it began to appear as if the Army of Northern Virginia was to be encircled.

Meanwhile, Lee was waiting only until he collected supplies and rations to last his men for a week and until the roads were passable before leaving to join Johnston. He hoped to leave on or about April 10. The information he received about the rapid accumulation of Union forces opposite his lightly held right was very disturbing, for it not only

Union soldiers on the ramparts of Confederate Fort Mahone, April 2, 1865. Courtesy, National Archives.

threatened to cut off his retreat to the west and south, but it also posed a serious danger to the Southside Railroad—the last remaining communication of Petersburg with the south, which continued to deliver a trickle of supplies to the city. So, while Sheridan was assembling his troops around Dinwiddie, Lee issued orders on March 29 which sent Generals George E. Pickett and Fitzhugh Lee to the Confederate right near Five Forks, far beyond Petersburg.

Sheridan was prepared to move against the Confederates with his cavalry on March 30, but heavy rains lasting from the evening of March 29 until the morning of the 31st made a large-scale movement impracticable over the unpaved roads. During the storm he kept his horses around Dinwiddie. On the last day of the month a portion of Sheridan's forces which had pushed northwest toward Five Forks were engaged by Southern forces who succeeded in driving them back toward the main Union troop concentration at Dinwiddie Court House. Pickett, the Confederate leader, then found his men badly outnumbered and withdrew them to Five Forks without pressing the advantage he had gained. This incident, often called the Battle of Dinwiddie Court House, was a minor Confederate victory, although Sheridan's men were neither demoralized nor disorganized by the attack, and Lee could find small comfort in the situation. Lee was able to concentrate on his right only about 10,600 cold and hungry Confederates to meet the expected Union drive to turn

A Union Army wagon train entering Petersburg. Courtesy, National Archives.

his right flank. Massed against him at this part of the line were more than 10,000 Northern cavalry and 43,000 infantry. The desperate urgency of Lee's fears was indicated in the dispatch he sent to Pickett early on April 1, the day of the struggle for Five Forks. *"Hold Five Forks at all hazards.* Protect road to Ford's Depot and prevent Union forces from striking the south-side railroad. Regret exceedingly your forced withdrawal, and your inability to hold the advantage you had gained."

Throughout April 1, Pickett's troops worked unceasingly, erecting barricades of logs, branches, and earth around Five Forks. At about 4 p. m., with only 2 hours of daylight remaining, Sheridan's cavalry and Warren's infantry attacked. While the dismounted cavalry charged the Confederates from the front of their newly erected defense line, two divisions of foot soldiers from the V Corps drove around to the left of Pickett's troops and, after crossing the White Oak Road which connected Five Forks with Petersburg, hit them on the weakly held left flank. Lacking sufficient artillery support, the Southerners were quickly overcome. Realizing that their position was no longer tenable, portions of the Confederate troops tried to retreat to Petersburg, but the avenue of escape had been cut by the Union advance across the White Oak Road.

By dusk, the Battle of Five Forks had ended. Union troops were in possession of the disputed area. They had cut off and captured over 3,200 prisoners, while suffering a loss which was probably less than 1,000.

Now the besieging forces had nearly succeeded in accomplishing Grant's objective of encircling the city. The western extremity of Lee's defenses had crumbled.

Those Confederates who survived the Battle of Five Forks had fallen back to the Southside Railroad where they rallied for a defensive stand, but darkness had prevented a Union pursuit. Grant's troops were within striking distance of the rail line, located less than 3 miles from Five Forks. Lee now knew that Petersburg must be evacuated without delay or the Army of Northern Virginia would be completely cut off from outside help and all possible escape routes would be gone.

The problem of assigning a proper significance to Five Forks is a difficult one. It is now known that Lee and the Confederate government officials were on the eve of the abandonment of their capital. In June of the previous year the Southside Railroad had been a most important objective of the invading army, but the plight of Lee's army had grown so desperate during the intervening months that whether the railroad remained open or not mattered little. Grant, of course, did not know this as a positive fact, although the uncomfortable situation of his opponents was something of which he was doubtless aware. The real importance of Five Forks lay in the probability that, by making it more difficult for Lee to escape, it brought the inevitable a little closer. Brig. Gen. Horace Porter, of Grant's staff, was positive more than 30 years later that news of Sheridan's success prompted the Union commander in chief to issue the orders for the attack that carried the city.

Maj. Gen. Philip H. Sheridan, Union commander at the Battle of Five Forks. Courtesy, National Archives.

The Fall of the City

Continuously throughout the night following the Battle of Five Forks, the Union artillery played upon the Confederate earthworks and dropped shells within the city. Troops were prepared for a large general assault which had been ordered for the following dawn. At 4:40 a. m., April 2, 1865, a wide frontal attack was begun with the sound of a signal gun from Fort Fisher. A heavy fog, however, prevented the action from gaining full momentum until after 7 a. m.

The story of the fighting along the Petersburg front on that spring Sunday is one of Union success over stout Confederate resistance. The Union VI Corps, under Gen. Horatio G. Wright, broke through the Confederate right and rushed on to the Southside Railroad. Other elements of Grant's army swept away the remnants of the Confederate lines along Hatcher's Run. Early in the day, Lt. Gen. Ambrose P. Hill, a Confederate corps commander, had been killed by the bullet of a Union soldier near the Boydton Plank Road when on the way to rally his men at Hatcher's Run.

The desperateness of the Southern position was shown when, about 10 a. m., Lee telegraphed President Davis to inform him of the turn events had taken at Petersburg. The message read: "I advise that all preparations be made for leaving Richmond tonight." Davis received the message while attending Sunday services at St. Paul's Church. He left immediately, destroying the calm of worship, in order to prepare for evacuating the capital. The flight of the Confederate government was promptly begun.

By midday the entire outer line to the west of Petersburg had been captured with the exception of Forts Gregg and Baldwin. The city was now completely surrounded except to the north. The left of the Union line finally rested on the bank of the Appomattox River after months of strenuous effort.

It now became apparent to Lee that he must hold an inner line west of Petersburg until nightfall, when it would be possible for him to retreat from the city. While gray-clad troops were forming along this line built on the banks of Old Indian Town Creek, the defenders of Forts Gregg and Baldwin put up a stubborn delaying action against the Northern advance. At Fort Gregg, particularly, there was a desperate Confederate defense. Approximately 300 men and 2 pieces of artillery met an onslaught of 5,000 Northerners. The outcome of the struggle was determined by the numbers in the attacking force, but the capture of Fort Gregg occurred only after bitter hand-to-hand combat. Fort Baldwin was forced to yield shortly after the fall of Fort Gregg. The purpose of the defense of these two positions had been accomplished, however, for a thin but sturdy line running behind them from Battery 45 to the Appomattox River had been manned. Temporarily, at least, street fighting within Petersburg had been avoided. Blows directed at this line at

The Crater area. The bank in the background is the original Confederate earthwork constructed in 1864.

other points, such as Fort Mahone near the southeast corner of the defense works, were turned back. Yet there was no doubt in the mind of Lee and other Southern leaders that all hope of retaining Petersburg and Richmond was gone. It was obvious that, if the lines held the Union Army in check on April 2, they must be surrendered on the morrow. The object was to delay until evening when retreat would be possible.

The close of the day found the weary Confederates concentrating within Petersburg and making all possible plans to withdraw. Lee had issued the necessary instructions at 3 o'clock that afternoon. By 8 p. m. the retreat was under way, the artillery preceding the infantry across the Appomattox River. Amelia Court House, 40 miles to the west, was designated as the assembly point for the troops from Petersburg and Richmond.

Grant had ordered the assault on Petersburg to be renewed early the next morning (April 3). It was discovered at 3 a. m. that the Southern earthworks had been abandoned, and so an attack was not necessary. Union troops took possession of the city shortly after 4 a. m. Richmond officially surrendered 4 hours later.

President Lincoln, who had been in the vicinity of Petersburg for several days, came from Army Headquarters at City Point that same day for a brief visit with Grant. They talked quietly on the porch of a private home for an hour and a half before the President returned to City Point. Grant with all of his army, except the detachments necessary to police

Petersburg and Richmond and to protect City Point, set out in immediate pursuit of Lee. He left Maj. Gen. George L. Hartsuff in command at Petersburg.

Petersburg had fallen, but it was at a heavy price. In the absence of complete records the exact casualties will never be known, but in the 10-month campaign at least 42,000 Union troops had been killed, wounded, and captured, while the Confederates had suffered losses of more than 28,000. Although the Northern forces had lost more men than their opponents, they had been able to replenish them more readily. Moreover, Grant had been prepared to utilize the greater resources at his disposal, and the Petersburg campaign had been turned by him into a form of relentless attrition which the Southern Army had not been able to stand. The result had been the capture of Petersburg and, more important, of the Southern capital. It had also resulted in the flight of the remnants of the once mighty Army of Northern Virginia.

On the Sunday following the evacuation of Petersburg and Richmond, Lee's troops at Appomattox Court House were cut off from any possibility of uniting with Johnston in North Carolina. In this small Virginia town, nearly 100 miles west of Petersburg, the Army of Northern Virginia, now numbering little more than 28,000, surrendered to the Union forces. Within a week of the fall of Petersburg the major striking force of the Confederacy had capitulated. The Civil War finally was all but ended. Gen. Joseph E. Johnston surrendered his army to General Sherman in North Carolina on April 26, 1865.

View from east to west across the Crater.

Please refer to your Official Park Map for a current list of tour stops.

Guide to the Area

A self-guided tour of Petersburg National Military Park may be made by automobile. This tour, extending 27 miles, begins at the Crater and park museum and follows the lines of earthworks around the city. It offers a nearly complete picture of the engagements which occurred during the campaign and gives an idea of the scope and magnitude of the area covered by the contending forces. Throughout the tour you will have an opportunity to study exhibits and narrative markers which will help you to orient yourself with the terrain.

In the description of the tour which follows an attempt has been made to provide you with a guide to all the important points of interest. The following remarks about this description may prove useful. The total road distances from the starting point at the Crater and park museum to the various points of interest are shown in parentheses. The distances are stated to the nearest tenth of a mile. All route numbers are State or county unless they are identified as United States highway routes. Points of historic interest are identified in capital letters (FORT FISHER, BATTERY PEGRAM, etc.) where they are mentioned for the first time. The numbers at the beginning of various paragraphs correspond to the circled numbers on the Park Tour Map found on pages 26–27.

1. The CRATER (0.0) is the scene of the Battle of the Crater, July 30, 1864. You may see the results of the explosion of the Union mine and the ground for which both armies contested. Information can be obtained at the park museum, where there is usually a member of the staff on duty. Talks on the Battle of the Crater and the Petersburg Campaign are given at frequent intervals. The museum contains exhibits pertinent to the fighting at Petersburg.

You should then follow the small "Park Tour" signs which will conduct you to Battery 5. Return to the junction of the Crater entrance with U. S. 460 and 301 (0.3). A *left turn* is made on this highway (called in 1864 the JERUSALEM PLANK ROAD) which is followed to the fork where U. S. 460 branches left (east) to Norfolk (0.5). Follow U. S. 460 across the bridge which spans the tracks of the Norfolk and Western Railroad. These tracks are on the same approximate roadbed used by the NORFOLK AND PETERSBURG RAILROAD in 1864–65. Continue across bridge to the intersection of Siege Road (1.3) which is identified by a large "Park Tour" sign. *Turn left* on Siege Road.

2. BATTERY 16 was located at the left of this intersection. This is one of many Union artillery emplacements constructed during the campaign. Similar batteries were constructed by the Confederates. Siege Road follows the Union lines east of Petersburg which were held from June 18, 1864, to April 2, 1865.

An interior view of the remains of Fort Stedman.

3. FORT MORTON (1.4). The site of this fort is a short distance past Battery 16 and on the left of Siege Road. This fort, obliterated after the war, was the place from which Gen. Ambrose E. Burnside directed the attack of the Union IX Corps during the Battle of the Crater. It was a strongly fortified position and considered by many contemporary observers as one of the best of the nearly 50 forts surrounding the city.

4. Union BATTERY 13 (1.7). The tour continues along Siege Road, passing the remains of this battery, which are to the left. The Union batteries were numbered consecutively, beginning with Battery 1 on the Appomattox River east of Petersburg and running south and west around the city. There were 42 of these Union batteries by the end of the campaign. In a like manner, the Confederate batteries were numbered starting at the river. In the original defense lines (the "Dimmock Line") there were 55 Confederate batteries.

Notice on the left of Siege Road, and at numerous other places throughout the tour, the low breastworks which connect the forts and batteries to make a long, continuous line. It was behind these that the enlisted men spent much of their time during the campaign.

5. FORT HASKELL (2.0), on the left of Siege Road, is one of the best preserved of the earthworks. The most important event in its history occurred on the morning of March 25, 1865, when the defense made here by Union troops helped turn the tide against the Confederates during the Battle of Fort Stedman. The moat, or ditch, around the embank-

47

ments was made more formidable at that time with the aid of sharpened stakes (fraise) or brush (abatis). Chevaux-de-frise (timbers with sharpened stakes driven through at right angles) may also have been placed outside the moat. Gabions (cylindrical wicker baskets) and sandbags were placed on the fortifications to protect them from shot and shell. All of these devices were used regularly by both armies.

Siege Road crosses the Union siege line a short distance beyond Fort Haskell so that the earthworks are now on the right (east) of you. The road leads through a ravine.

6. BATTERY 11 (2.3) is situated at the top of the rise from the ravine. This, along with BATTERY 12 (since destroyed), was captured by the Confederates in the Battle of Fort Stedman, March 25, 1865. In the course of the engagement that followed, the battery changed hands several times. After the final Southern withdrawal that same day, the battery remained in Northern possession until the end of the war.

7. FORT STEDMAN (2.4) is close to Battery 11. The site is marked by well-preserved remains. This Union fort was the place selected by Confederate General Gordon for his attack on Grant's supply line. This attack occurred only 15 days before Lee surrendered at Appomattox Court House and was the last large-scale offensive movement of the Army of Northern Virginia. Although captured by the Confederates shortly after 4 a. m. on March 25, 1865, it was regained by the Northern forces within 4 hours. Fort Stedman also stands on the site of heavy fighting on June 18, 1864, when Grant failed to break the defense line that had been built the night before. However, the fort was not constructed until a month following this opening battle. Inside the fort is a monument erected by the State of Pennsylvania to the memory of the 3d Division, IX Corps, Army of the Potomac, which participated in the Battle of Fort Stedman.

Battery 5 on the original Confederate defense line, captured by Union forces on June 15, 1864.

Monument to Col. George W. Gowen, 48th Pennsylvania Regiment, killed in the assault on Fort Mahone, April 2, 1865.

Twenty-five yards past the Fort Stedman trailside exhibit, *turn left* on Sortie Road. This road passes between the lines and indicates their proximity at this point.

8. The MAINE MONUMENT may be seen near the bottom of the gentle slope on the right (north) of Sortie Road. This marks the scene of the heaviest fighting on June 18, 1864. At this point the 1st Maine Heavy Artillery suffered the heavy casualties referred to in the text.

9. COLQUITT'S SALIENT (2.6) is reached after traversing the short distance between the lines. This fortified position was named for Confederate Gen. A. H. Colquitt. It was one of the closest to the Union lines and was selected by Gordon as the place from which to launch the attack of March 25, 1865.

10. GRACIE'S DAM ruins (2.8) are behind Colquitt's Salient. This dam was one of several constructed by the Confederates around the city in order to flood the ground between the lines and prevent a surprise attack.

The tour continues around Colquitt's Salient and back to Siege Road. A *left turn* is made on Siege Road where it is followed by a *right turn* on PRINCE GEORGE COURT HOUSE ROAD (3.2) 50 yards north. This road is a colonial stage route which connected Petersburg with Prince George Court House. Part of the road has been restored. It leads east behind the Union siege line and in the general direction of Grant's supply base at City Point.

11. HARRISON'S CREEK (3.5) is the major point of historic interest on this road. On the banks of this stream the Confederate drive of March 25, 1865, was checked by a Union artillery barrage from a low ridge to the east followed by charges of Blue-clad infantry.

Continue straight on Prince George Court House Road to Attack Road (4.1). This is the first intersection past Harrison's Creek.

12. BATTERY 9. The partially destroyed remains of this battery may be seen across Attack Road. This Confederate artillery position was part of the "Dimmock Line." It was captured by Union troops advancing from the north in the early evening of June 15, 1864. About one-third of a mile southeast of this point Prince George Court House Road crossed Grant's military railroad. MEADE'S STATION, an important Union supply and hospital depot, was located at this intersection.

A *left turn* is made on Attack Road. The tour now travels north along the site of the original Confederate line ("Dimmock Line").

13. BATTERY 8 (4.5) lies to the left of a sharp curve in Attack Road. This Confederate battery, like Battery 9, was part of the line which fell on June 15, 1864. It was turned into a Union artillery post named FORT FRIEND and, ironically, guns placed here by the Northerners were used to repel the Confederates who had broken the line at Fort Stedman. The spires of Petersburg may be seen about 2½ miles west of Battery 8.

Continue on Attack Road to the intersection (4.9) with State Route 36 (Petersburg-Hopewell Road). *Turn right* on this highway and continue to the *entrance to the park on the left*. This entrance is marked by a large "Petersburg National Military Park" sign (5.1). *Turn left* on this road.

14. BATTERY 5 (5.4) is located at the end of this short park road. This is another of the original Confederate works which fell on the evening of June 15. The Union Army renamed it BATTERY 4. You may follow a path through the battery and observe the commanding position it held against attack from the north and east. Grant's troops overcame this by slipping around to the southwest and entering it there. This path also leads to a full-size replica of the large siege mortar known as "THE DICTATOR," or "THE PETERSBURG EXPRESS." This huge 17,000-pound, 13-inch mortar shelled Petersburg from the approximate position where the replica now stands.

To continue the tour proceed on Mortar Road, which encircles Battery 5, and brings you back to State Route 36 (1 mile). Retrace your route from this point to the intersection (10.7) of U. S. 460 and 301.

At the intersection of U. S. 460 and 301A *turn left* on U. S. 301 and continue to intersection (11.8) with U. S. 301A.

15. The GOWEN MONUMENT erected in honor of Col. George W. Gowen, a Union officer from Pennsylvania, who was killed on the last day of battle at Petersburg, April 2, 1865, stands at the right of this intersection.

16. "FORT HELL" (FORT SEDGWICK) of the Union line may be seen on the left of U. S. 301, a short distance past the Gowen Monument. It was given its nickname because of the heavy Confederate artillery fire, which was concentrated there when the fort was begun. Fort Sedgwick is now privately owned.

17. FORT DAVIS. Continue on U. S. 301 until you come to this fort, on the right of the highway (12.5). It is one of the best remaining examples of Union works. Near here Grant launched his first attack on the WELDON RAILROAD on June 21–22, 1864, but was driven back. Within the fort, evidences of "bombproofs" and traversing trenches still exist.

Turn right on to Flank Road at Fort Davis. This follows the Union siege lines south and southwest of Petersburg. Low breastworks still remain between the forts and batteries in many places.

18. FORT ALEXANDER HAYS (13.5). On the right of Flank Road may be seen the almost completely obliterated remains of this fort. It was built in August and September of 1864.

19. Union BATTERY 24 (13.9) stands on the left of Flank Road. This, like other batteries on both sides, was very active during the siege operations. It participated in the final artillery barrage during the night of April 1–2, 1865.

20. BATTERY 25 (14.4) will next be seen as you continue driving to the west on the tour.

21. The site of FORT HOWARD is approximately one-third of a mile beyond Battery 25, although not visible from the tour route. At Battery 25 the Union line crosses Flank Road and continues north, or right, of the road.

22. BATTERY 26 (15.3), like Battery 25, is found on the left. Near this battery Flank Road recrosses the earthworks.

The next important landmark after passing Battery 26 is the junction (16.0) of Flank Road with State Route 604 (Halifax Road). In front of you is the monument to Johnson Hagood's South Carolina brigade, and Fort Wadsworth.

23. FORT WADSWORTH stands on the left, a short distance past this intersection. This was a strategically located position for the Union Army, as it was close to the tracks of the Weldon Railroad. In this vicin-

ity, but before Fort Wadsworth was built, the Battle of Globe Tavern was fought on August 18–21, 1864. The site of GLOBE TAVERN is about one-half mile southeast of Fort Wadsworth. Globe Tavern was Gen. G. K. Warren's headquarters during the August battle.

Directly west of Fort Wadsworth, Flank Road underpasses the Atlantic Coast Line Railroad. The tour continues straight west, following Union infantry breastworks on the left, to the intersection (16.7) with State Route 675. State Route 675 may be found mentioned in Civil War dispatches as VAUGHAN ROAD. A *left turn* is made on State Route 675.

24. The POPLAR GROVE NATIONAL CEMETERY entrance (16.2) is identified by a marker. *Turn left* on to the cemetery grounds. Poplar Grove is situated on ground captured by the Union Army in the fight for the Weldon Railroad, August 18–21. In the winter of 1864–65, the 50th New York Engineers, encamped here, constructed a large log church. The cemetery contains the graves of more than 6,000 soldiers and veterans, of which over 4,000 are unknown. Nearly all are Union veterans of the Civil War.

After a drive through the cemetery grounds the tour returns to State Route 675 (17.9). *Turn right* and drive north to the junction (18.3) with State Route 676 which intersects 675 on the left. A *turn* is made on Route 676. That route is followed to the end, where it connects with State Route 613 (19.1), known to history as the SQUIRREL LEVEL ROAD.

The moat and embankments of Union Fort Davis.

25. Union FORT URMSTON was constructed in the autumn and early winter of 1864 on the west side of the Squirrel Level Road. It was named in honor of a Union officer killed at the Battle of Peebles' Farm (September 29–October 1, 1864). The heaviest fighting of this engagement took place around Peebles' Farm, three-quarters of a mile southwest of here.

Turn left on State Route 613 and continue to the intersection (19.6) with State Route 672 (CHURCH ROAD). State Route 672 is the right fork at this intersection. *Turn* on this road and continue in a northwest direction.

26. FORT FISHER (20.3) is situated on the right side of the road. This Union stronghold is in an excellent state of preservation, and it is one of the largest earthen forts constructed in the Civil War. Fort Fisher played an important part in the campaign after it was built in late 1864. Near it was a 150-foot Union watchtower used to observe enemy movements and to spot artillery fire. Behind it, a short distance to the south, was a field of execution for military offenders and spies where, according to one observer, violators paid the supreme penalty nearly every week. It was a signal gun from Fort Fisher which boomed the beginning of the final assault on the defenses of Petersburg, April 2, 1865.

27. FORTS WELCH and GREGG. On the left of the road the Union line continues to these forts, the remains of which are not visible from the road.

The tour is resumed on State Route 672, or Church Road. This runs from the Union to the Confederate line. The road crosses the tracks of the Seaboard Air Line Railroad and, later, overpasses the Norfolk and Western Beltline Railroad. The direction of the tour is north toward the Appomattox River (21.8). *Turn right* at the intersection with State Route 603 and continue to the end of State Route 672 (21.3) where it intersects State Route 142. This road (142) was named the BOYDTON PLANK ROAD at the time of the siege. *Turn right* on State Route 142. The direction of the tour is east along the Confederate defense line which was built south of Petersburg.

28. Confederate FORT GREGG (22.4). The partially destroyed remains of this fort are located nearly opposite a Union fort of the same name. Fort Gregg is situated about 100 yards to the left, or north, of the highway. It is memorable for the desperate struggle it put up against the Union attack on April 2, 1865. When it fell, the last Confederate stronghold on the outer line west of the city was in Northern hands.

29. FORT LEE (23.3). Continue on State Route 142 to this fort and junction with Park Road (Defense Road) on the right. Originally Battery 45 on the "Dimmock Line," Fort Lee was renamed in honor of the Confederate commander in chief. It was successfully held after the outer line

Poplar Grove National Cemetery.

fell on April 2, but was evacuated when the Confederates fled from Petersburg that night.

Turn right on Defense Road at Fort Lee and continue to the junction (23.8) with the Squirrel Level Road (State Route 613). On the right, or south, of Defense Road may be seen the remains of Confederate breastworks. *Cross* Squirrel Level Road and follow Defense Road. A short distance past this intersection the route underpasses the Atlantic Coast Line Railroad. After winding through a stand of tall pine trees, Defense Road merges with City Park Road (25.0).

30. BATTERY PEGRAM, an important Confederate artillery position, lies 100 yards to the right of this point.

The tour continues straight on City Park Road, which is a continuation of Defense Road. This curves through a ravine and, on the right, as the ascent from the ravine is begun, is Wilcox Lake, owned by the city of Petersburg.

31. FORT WALKER (25.5) is at the top of the hill. This, like Fort Lee, was taken by the Union troops after Lee's withdrawal during the night of April 2–3, 1865.

At Fort Walker, City Park Road *merges* with South Boulevard. This street approximates the Confederate defense line and now passes through the Walnut Hill section of Petersburg. Follow South Boulevard to the junction (26.6) with South Sycamore Street (U. S. 301).

Interior of Confederate Fort Mahone as it looked shortly after its capture in April 1865. Courtesy, National Archives.

32. Confederate FORT MAHONE was situated near the large Pennsylvania Monument which is visible 150 yards to the right of this intersection. This fort was the scene of heavy fighting on April 2, 1865.

You may turn on South Sycamore Street if you so desire. A right turn will lead toward Emporia, Va.; a left turn north toward Richmond.

Cross South Sycamore Street and continue on South Boulevard to intersection (26.8) with U. S. 301. *Turn left* on U. S. 301 and return to the Crater (28.0) and park museum where tour commenced.

In addition to these tours you may follow U. S. 1 south to the point where Gen. A. P. Hill fell, and on to Hatcher's Run, Burgess' Mill, and Dinwiddie Court House. These, and other important historical points, are identified by Virginia State historical markers. Four miles south of U. S. 460, west of Petersburg, is the Five Forks Battlefield where the fight occurred on April 1, 1865. The point closest to it on U. S. 460 is also indicated by a Virginia marker.

How To Reach the Park

The city of Petersburg, 23 miles south of Richmond, Va., is on U. S. 1, 301, 301A, and 460 and may also be reached by railroad or bus. Petersburg National Military Park lies southeast of the city. You are advised to begin your tour of the park by first going to the Crater and park museum. They may be reached by U. S. 301 and 460.

Administration

Petersburg National Military Park, established by act of Congress approved July 3, 1926, has a gross acreage of more than 1,500. It is a part of the National Park System owned by the people of the United States and administered for them by the National Park Service of the Department of the Interior. Communications and inquiries should be addressed to the Superintendent, Petersburg National Military Park, Petersburg, Va.

Related Areas

There are numerous other Civil War battlefields located in Virginia within easy driving distance of Petersburg National Military Park. Among them are Manassas and Richmond National Battlefield Parks and Fredericksburg and Spotsylvania National Military Park. The site of the surrender of Lee and the Army of Northern Virginia to Grant and his Union forces is also commemorated by Appomattox Court House National Historical Park.

Two important battles outside the boundaries of Virginia in which the Army of Northern Virginia engaged were at Antietam National Battlefield Site, Md., and Gettysburg National Military Park, Pa. These areas are also administered by the National Park Service for the benefit of the people of the United States.

Visitor Facilities

For the visitor's convenience and information, the park offers the following facilities and services: extensive drives and foot trails marked with interpretive devices; a field museum and library which is located in the Museum and Administration Building at the Crater; and frequent talks on the Battle of the Crater and the Petersburg Campaign.

DSI's New Releases: Civil War Battlefield Guides

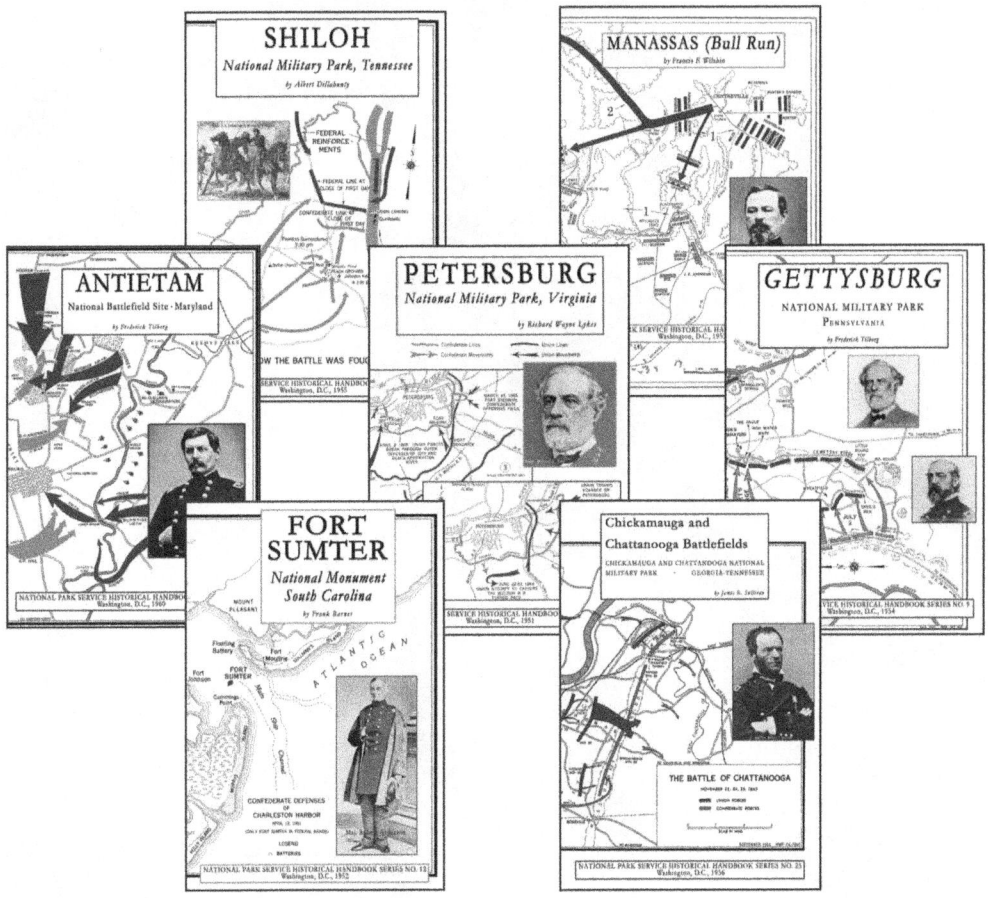

ISBN	Title	Page Count	Price
1582187770	Manassas (Bull Run)	56	$8.95
1582187789	Chickamauga and Chattanooga Battlefields	72	$8.95
1582187800	Gettysburg National Military Park	60	$8.95
1582187819	Shiloh National Military Park, Tennessee	58	$8.95
1582187827	Antietam National Battlefield Site, Maryland	72	$8.95
1582187835	Petersburg National Military Park, Virginia	68	$8.95
1582187843	Fort Sumter National Monument, South Carolina	56	$8.95

To order visit:
www.PDFLibrary.com

www.ingramcontent.com/pod-product-compliance
Lightning Source LLC
Chambersburg PA
CBHW031426040426
42444CB00006B/699